S-T-E-M IS EVERYWHERE!

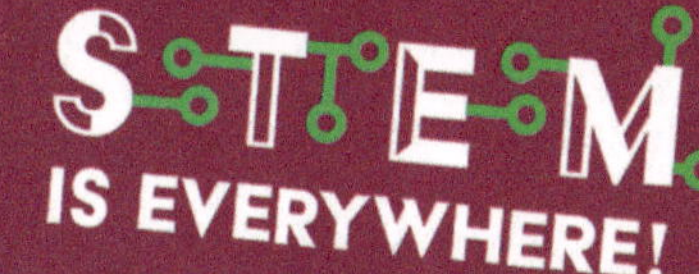

SELF-DRIVING CARS

TRANSPORTATION OF THE FUTURE

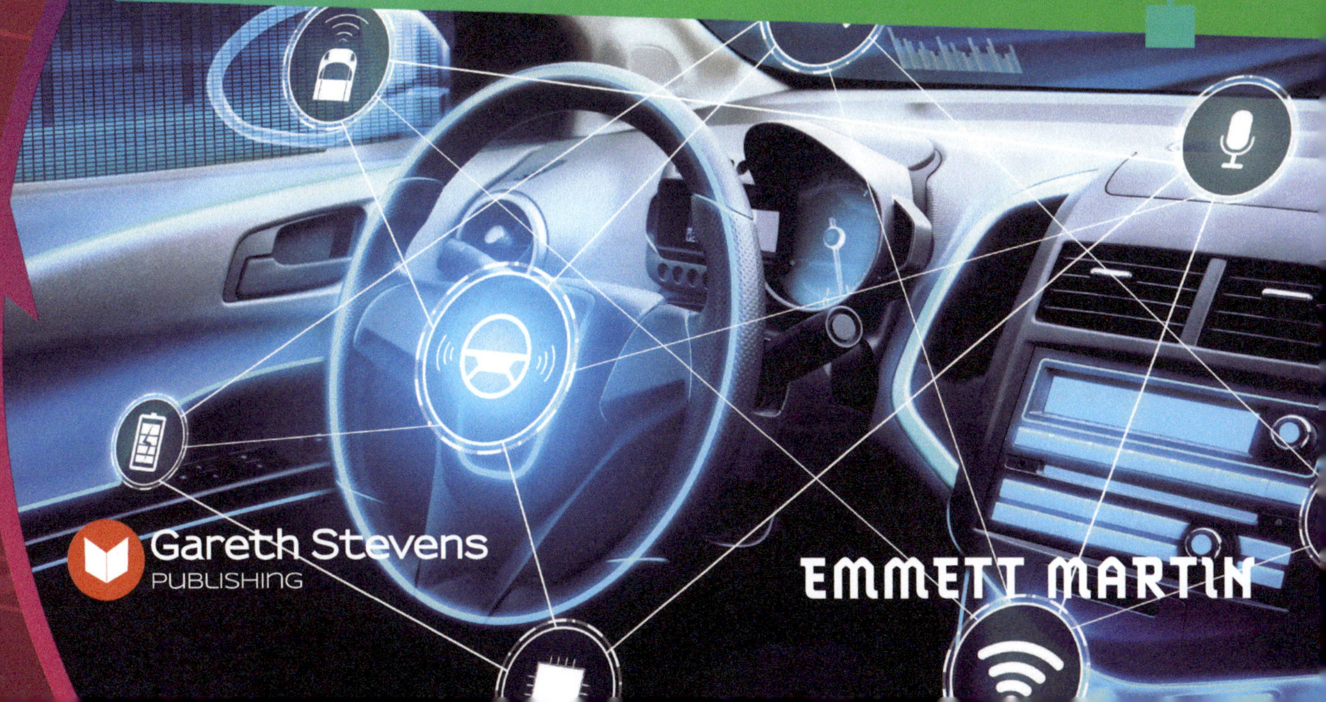

Gareth Stevens PUBLISHING

EMMETT MARTIN

**Please visit our website, www.garethstevens.com.
For a free color catalog of all our high-quality books,
call toll free 1-800-542-2595 or fax 1-877-542-2596.**

Portions of this work were originally authored by Ian Chow-Miller and published as *How Self-Driving Cars Work* (Everyday STEM). All new material in this edition authored by Emmett Martin.

Library of Congress Cataloging-in-Publication Data
Names: Martin, Emmett, author.
Title: Self-driving cars : transportation of the future / Emmett Martin.
Description: New York : Gareth Stevens Publishing, [2023] | Series: STEM is everywhere! | Includes index.
Identifiers: LCCN 2022022700 (print) | LCCN 2022022701 (ebook) | ISBN 9781538283578 (library binding) | ISBN 9781538283554 (paperback) | ISBN 9781538283585 (ebook)
Subjects: LCSH: Automated vehicles–Juvenile literature. | Automobiles–Automatic control–Juvenile literature. | Automated vehicles–Design and construction–Juvenile literature. | CYAC: Autonomous vehicles. | Automobiles.
Classification: LCC TL152.8 .M3725 2023 (print) | LCC TL152.8 (ebook) | DDC 629.2–dc23/eng/20220706
LC record available at https://lccn.loc.gov/2022022700
LC ebook record available at https://lccn.loc.gov/2022022701

Published in 2023 by
Gareth Stevens Publishing
2544 Clinton Street
Buffalo, NY 14224

Designer: Tanya Dellaccio
Editor: Therese Shea

Photo credits: Series Art Supphachai Salaeman/Shutterstock.com; cover Blue Planet Studio/Shutterstock.com; p. 4 LightField Studios/Shutterstock.com; p. 5 SariMe/Shutterstock.com; p. 7 https://upload.wikimedia.org/wikipedia/commons/5/59/Street_intersection_Futurama.jpg; p. 8 https://upload.wikimedia.org/wikipedia/commons/e/ee/Google_driverless_car_at_intersection.gk.jpg; p. 9 VanderWolf Images/Shutterstock.com; p. 10 ambrozinio/Shutterstock.com; p. 11 stockwerk-fotodesign/Shutterstock.com; p. 13 Scharfsinn/Shutterstock.com; p. 14 aslysun/Shutterstock.com; p. 15 Bob Pool/Shutterstock.com; p. 17 https://upload.wikimedia.org/wikipedia/commons/6/6e/Self_driving_Uber_prototype_in_San_Francisco.jpg; p. 19 https://upload.wikimedia.org/wikipedia/commons/b/be/Cruise_Automation_Bolt_EV_third_generation_in_San_Francisco.jpg; p. 21 EpicStockMedia/Shutterstock.com; p. 23 metamorworks/Shutterstock.com; p. 25 Southworks/Shutterstock.com; p. 27 Scharfsinn/Shutterstock.com.

Printed in the United States of America

CPSIA compliance information: Batch #CWGS23: For further information contact Gareth Stevems Publishing at 1-800-398-2504.

CONTENTS

Words in the glossary appear in **bold** type the first time they are used in the text.

BUCKLE UP!

We're used to hopping in a **vehicle** and getting to where we need to go fast, perhaps school, soccer practice, music lessons, or a family visit. Our parents or another caregiver might do the driving. And they're probably so familiar with driving that using the turn signals, pressing on the gas or brake pedals, and turning the steering wheel doesn't take too much thought.

IN THE FUTURE, THE PERSON IN THE DRIVER'S SEAT OF A SELF-DRIVING CAR WILL HAVE MUCH LESS TO DO!

CATCH THIS BUS

CARS AREN'T THE ONLY DRIVERLESS VEHICLES BEING DEVELOPED. PERHAPS WHERE YOU LIVE YOU TAKE THE BUS RATHER THAN A CAR. MANY PEOPLE IN CITIES DEPEND ON BUSES TO GET AROUND. DRIVERLESS BUSES, TOO, ARE BEING TESTED IN CITIES AROUND THE WORLD, INCLUDING LAS VEGAS, NEVADA, AND PROVIDENCE, RHODE ISLAND.

Soon, the act of driving may change for many families. Carmakers are creating vehicles that drive themselves. These cars don't need a person to drive them. Many don't even need steering wheels! Read on to learn more about the **technology** behind self-driving cars.

IN THE BEGINNING

The idea of self-driving vehicles isn't new. At the 1939 World's Fair in New York City, the General Motors car company and **designer** Norman Bel Geddes created an exhibit meant to show what the future would look like. The display revealed a city with tall buildings, wide roads, and cars that were controlled by radio waves.

In the 1950s, the Radio Corporation of America (RCA) and General Motors experimented with cars on "controlled highways, " which had wires in the roadways. A car with a machine that could detect the electricity in the wires could travel down the road without the driver touching the steering wheel.

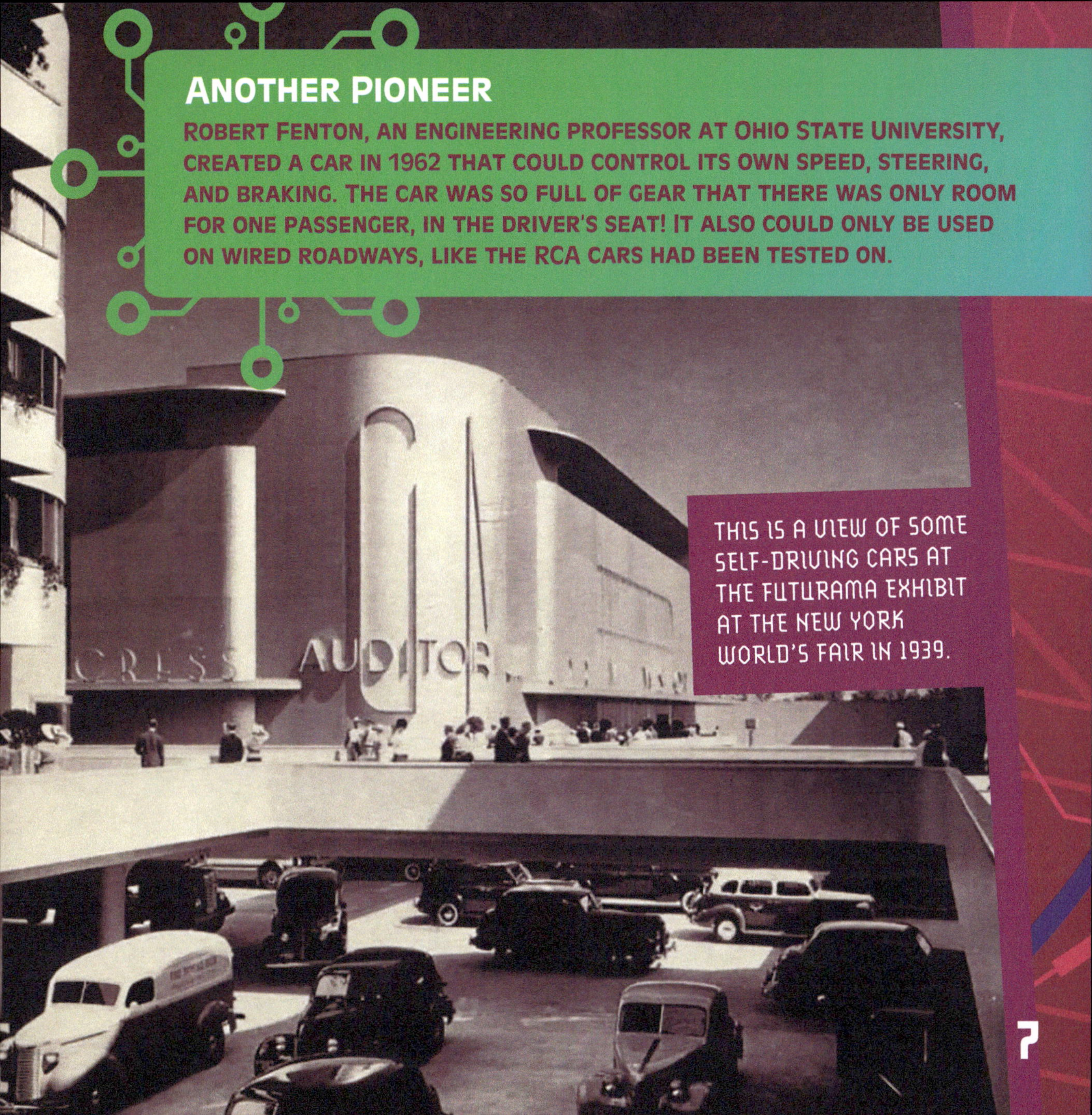

ANOTHER PIONEER

ROBERT FENTON, AN ENGINEERING PROFESSOR AT OHIO STATE UNIVERSITY, CREATED A CAR IN 1962 THAT COULD CONTROL ITS OWN SPEED, STEERING, AND BRAKING. THE CAR WAS SO FULL OF GEAR THAT THERE WAS ONLY ROOM FOR ONE PASSENGER, IN THE DRIVER'S SEAT! IT ALSO COULD ONLY BE USED ON WIRED ROADWAYS, LIKE THE RCA CARS HAD BEEN TESTED ON.

THIS IS A VIEW OF SOME SELF-DRIVING CARS AT THE FUTURAMA EXHIBIT AT THE NEW YORK WORLD'S FAIR IN 1939.

AUTONOMY

Today, we don't think of self-driving cars as needing wired highways. We think of them as being much more like robots that can respond to any road by themselves. But not all self-driving cars work completely by themselves. Some need the driver to help control their movements. The amount of control a car has over its movements is called autonomy.

A FRIENDLY LOOK

THE GOOGLE COMPANY HAS BEEN ONE OF THE LEADERS IN MODERN SELF-DRIVING TECHNOLOGY. IN 2014, IT ANNOUNCED IT WAS MAKING TWO-SEATED AUTONOMOUS CARS WITH A FRONT THAT LOOKED A BIT LIKE A SMILING FACE. THE COMPANY SAID IT WANTED PEOPLE TO FEEL RELAXED WHEN THEY SAW A CAR WITHOUT A DRIVER.

THIS IS THE INSIDE OF A MERCEDES-BENZ AUTONOMOUS **CONCEPT CAR**.

Some self-driving cars have a lot of autonomy. A car with full autonomy drives itself without any help. There's no driver and no steering wheel or pedals. The car can start, stop, speed up, slow down, turn, and park on its own.

Some cars on the road today aren't fully autonomous but have autonomous controls. They use assistive devices, which means the car assists the driver. The car may do this by warning the driver in a dangerous situation. If another car gets too close, the assistive device may beep, for example. The driver needs to slow down or steer away from the danger.

CARMAKERS COLLECT DATA FROM VEHICLES TO LEARN HOW TO IMPROVE AUTONOMOUS CONTROL SYSTEMS.

STAYING BETWEEN THE LINES

ANOTHER ASSISTIVE DEVICE IS CALLED LANE-ASSIST TECHNOLOGY. WHEN THE CAR DETECTS THAT IT'S DRIFTING OVER THE LINES OF THE ROAD, IT MAY GIVE A WARNING BEEP. SOME CARS CAN TAKE OVER STEERING TO CORRECT THE VEHICLE'S COURSE. THIS IS HELPFUL IF THE DRIVER IS FALLING ASLEEP OR NOT LOOKING AT THE ROAD FOR ANOTHER REASON.

More and more cars have an autonomous **emergency** braking system that acts when the car detects something in its path. For example, it might brake when someone is crossing the road in front of the vehicle or when the car is backing into another vehicle in a parking lot.

HOW DO SELF-DRIVING CARS WORK?

So, how do autonomous cars, or those with at least some autonomous control, work? Have you ever seen a smartphone telling a driver where to go? A computer program inside the phone lets it do this. A **navigation** program works using GPS, which stands for "Global Positioning System."

The GPS in a phone receives signals from **satellites**. Satellites orbit Earth, moving at a steady speed. The phone compares the signals from several different satellites. This lets it locate itself (and the car it's in) on a map. The phone uses GPS to track and guide the car as it moves. Self-driving cars use GPS technology too.

BUILT IN

IN A SELF-DRIVING CAR, A COMPUTER WITH A GPS PROGRAM IS BUILT INTO THE CAR. THE COMPUTER CONTROLS GPS AND OTHER SYSTEMS IN THE CAR. GPS SIGNALS CAN GET LOST IN CITIES WITH TALL BUILDINGS. CONDITIONS IN THE ATMOSPHERE CAN DISRUPT SIGNALS TOO. AUTONOMOUS CARMAKERS ARE COMING UP WITH NEW SOLUTIONS FOR THESE PROBLEMS.

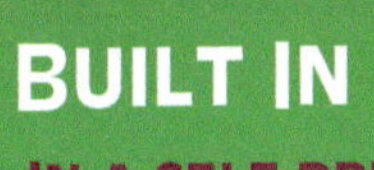

THE U.S. GOVERNMENT OWNS AND MAINTAINS GPS, WHICH USES AT LEAST 24 SATELLITES THAT ORBIT EARTH TWICE DAILY.

SENSING ITS SURROUNDINGS

Think of what a truly self-driving car must do to get somewhere safely. It must avoid all dangers that come into its path. These dangers include other cars on the road as well as animals and human beings that might be in the way.

A LOT TO THINK ABOUT

SOME PEOPLE THINK TRAFFIC WILL GET WORSE WHEN WE HAVE A LOT OF SELF-DRIVING CARS ON THE ROAD. WHY? PEOPLE MIGHT SEND THEIR CARS OUT TO GET SUPPLIES OR HAVE THEM CIRCLE THE BLOCK INSTEAD OF PAYING FOR PARKING! AUTONOMOUS CARS WILL HAVE IMPACTS THAT WE MIGHT NOT EVEN IMAGINE.

A SELF-DRIVING CAR WILL NEED TO KNOW TO SLOW DOWN IN A WORK ZONE AND DRIVE AROUND **OBSTACLES** IN ITS WAY.

A self-driving car needs to know the difference between a bicycle and a motorcycle. It needs to know if it is approaching a stoplight or a stop sign. It needs to know if anyone is standing in a parking space. How does the driverless car know all of these things? It uses information, or data, from its sensors.

Sensors are devices that "sense" information about the **environment** around them and send that information to a computer. Sensors are similar to the parts of your body that sense: Your ears hear sounds and your eyes see images, for example. Your brain uses this information to help your body respond to what's going on around it. Sensors in self-driving cars take in sounds and images as well and send them as data to the car's computer.

Camera sensors are one kind. They have to be mounted at every angle around the car to take in a complete view.

WEATHER WORRIES

CAMERA SENSORS ALONE AREN'T ENOUGH TO DETECT WHAT'S AROUND A CAR, THOUGH. WEATHER CONDITIONS SUCH AS THICK FOG AND HEAVY SNOW CAN MAKE IT HARD FOR DRIVERS TO SEE OBSTACLES THEY'RE APPROACHING. CAMERA SENSORS IN SELF-DRIVING CARS HAVE THE SAME PROBLEM. MORE KINDS OF SENSORS ARE NEEDED FOR WHEN CAMERAS FAIL.

YOU CAN SEE THE MANY CAMERA SENSORS MOUNTED AROUND THIS AUTONOMOUS VEHICLE.

LIDAR

Lidar is another kind of sensor used in some autonomous vehicles. "Lidar" stands for "light detection and ranging." Lidar shoots out laser light in thousands of quick pulses, or bursts, per second. Then, a receiver in the car waits for those pulses to bounce back. That data, along with a special computer program, can create 3D models of objects around the car.

These laser light pulses are different from laser guns you may have seen in movies or on TV. They're invisible and can't hurt people. All together, they can help cars "see" objects around them.

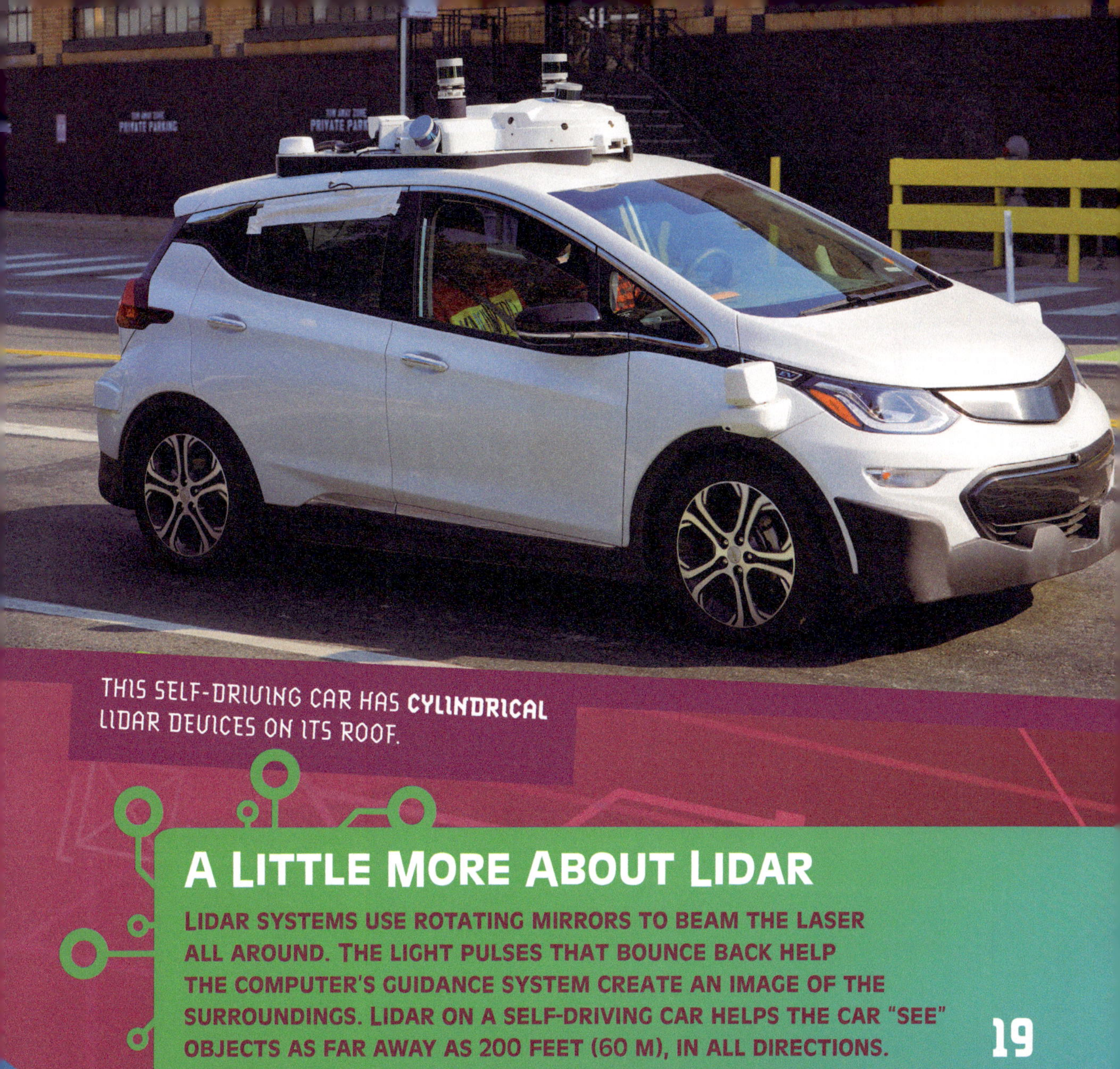

THIS SELF-DRIVING CAR HAS **CYLINDRICAL** LIDAR DEVICES ON ITS ROOF.

A LITTLE MORE ABOUT LIDAR

LIDAR SYSTEMS USE ROTATING MIRRORS TO BEAM THE LASER ALL AROUND. THE LIGHT PULSES THAT BOUNCE BACK HELP THE COMPUTER'S GUIDANCE SYSTEM CREATE AN IMAGE OF THE SURROUNDINGS. LIDAR ON A SELF-DRIVING CAR HELPS THE CAR "SEE" OBJECTS AS FAR AWAY AS 200 FEET (60 M), IN ALL DIRECTIONS.

SONAR

Self-driving cars may also use sonar, which stands for "sound navigation and ranging." Sonar technology is similar to lidar. But instead of using laser pulses like lidar does, sonar uses sound waves to locate objects. Active sonar emits, or sends out, sound waves, which echo back to a receiver after they hit a solid object. The timing of the echoes communicate to the car's computer how far away that object is.

IT'S ULTRASONIC

ULTRASONIC SENSORS USE SOUND WAVES OF A **FREQUENCY** ABOVE HUMAN HEARING. THEY'RE USED TO ASSIST WITH PARKING. THEY'RE ALSO USED TO DETECT OBJECTS IN A CAR'S "BLIND SPOT." THIS IS AN AREA ON THE ROAD THAT CANNOT BE SEEN BY A DRIVER LOOKING AT SIDE AND REARVIEW MIRRORS.

THE TESLA MODEL S HAS 12 ULTRASONIC UNITS IN ITS FRONT AND REAR BUMPERS. THESE SENSORS WORK BEST TO DETECT OBJECTS CLOSE TO A CAR.

Sonar in self-driving cars is similar to animals' **echolocation**. Bats and dolphins use echolocation to find their way as well as to sense predators and prey around them.

THE COMPLETE PICTURE

Lidar produces 360-degree maps, or a whole circle, of the area around the vehicle. And while lidar can detect signs and traffic lights, self-driving cars need cameras too. Lidar can detect shapes, but a camera is needed to sense colors (and read speed limits and other words and numbers).

Bad weather affects lidar's performance. Radar and sonar can still work well in these conditions, but they can't create an accurate, or exact, shape of an object or a map like lidar can. That's why autonomous cars employ more than one kind of sensor, to reduce errors in all sorts of driving situations.

AND RADAR TOO

ANOTHER SENSOR FEATURED IN AUTONOMOUS CARS IS RADAR. "RADAR" STANDS FOR "RADIO DETECTION AND RANGING." THIS TECHNOLOGY USES ANTENNAE TO EMIT RADIO WAVES TO FIND SURROUNDING OBJECTS. RADAR, TOO, CAN ESTABLISH THE DISTANCE TO A DETECTED OBJECT AS WELL AS THE OBJECT'S SPEED IF IT'S MOVING.

CAR CONCERNS

In 2021, about 42,915 people died in vehicle crashes in the United States. Many of those deaths were linked to human error. Self-driving cars could avoid some mistakes that lead to accidents. Still, people have concerns about self-driving cars.

One argument is that autonomous cars will take away jobs. For example, self-driving trucks and buses could put truck drivers and bus drivers out of work.

Another problem is figuring out who's at fault after an accident. Between July 2021 and May 2022, 392 crashes of vehicles with partially autonomous driver-assist systems were reported. Is the car owner, the car company, or the maker of the sensors to blame?

Many car accidents occur because people are **distracted** while driving, such as texting or talking on the phone. In a self-driving car, it wouldn't matter if passengers were distracted.

A Human Advantage

Human drivers can do better than self-driving cars in bad weather. It's really tough for an autonomous car's computer to know how to drive in rain, ice, and snow. And this weather isn't ideal for some kinds of sensors either. So this is one area in which experienced drivers still have an advantage—for now.

GIVING UP CONTROL

Control is another obstacle in the way of self-driving cars. People have been driving cars for more than 100 years. For all that time, drivers have been in control. Being in control gives people a feeling of safety. When people aren't in control, they often feel helpless or nervous. It may take people a long time to get used to cars that control themselves.

However, with more and more vehicles having some autonomous features, such as emergency braking and lane-assist systems, people may grow accustomed to giving up control a little bit at a time.

WOULD YOU FEEL COMFORTABLE RIDING IN AN AUTONOMOUS CAR?

LEVEL UP

THE SOCIETY OF AUTOMOTIVE ENGINEERS (SAE) USES A SYSTEM TO DESCRIBE THE DEGREE OF AUTONOMY A CAR MAY HAVE. IN LEVEL 0, A DRIVER HAS NO ASSISTANCE. IN LEVELS 1 AND 2, THE CAR OFFERS SOME ASSISTING TECHNOLOGY, BUT THE DRIVER MUST BE IN CONTROL. IN LEVELS 3, 4, AND 5, THE CAR CAN TAKE CONTROL OF DRIVING.

TRANSPORTING US INTO THE FUTURE

As of mid-2022, fully autonomous cars cannot be purchased and driven in the United States, though they are being tested daily. However, the U.S. National Highway Traffic Safety Administration announced in 2022 that carmakers could begin designing and making cars that don't have steering wheels and pedals. This paves the way for truly autonomous vehicles on the roads in the near future.

The technology of self-driving cars continues to improve each year. No doubt, when they're finally available for all, autonomous cars will change lives—and hopefully even save them. Will you be one of the people cheering on this technology?

SELF-DRIVING TECHNOLOGY TIMELINE

1478 LEONARDO DA VINCI DRAWS PLANS FOR A SELF-DRIVING CART.

1939 NORMAN BEL GEDDES AND GENERAL MOTORS CREATE AN EXHIBIT AT THE NEW YORK WORLD'S FAIR SUGGESTING SELF-DRIVING CARS AS A FUTURE TECHNOLOGY.

1957 RCA AND GENERAL MOTORS DEVELOP A CAR THAT CAN SENSE ELECTRICAL SIGNALS FROM SPECIAL WIRES IN THE ROAD.

1979 A STANFORD UNIVERSITY SCIENTIST SENDS A SELF-DRIVING CART SAFELY ACROSS A ROOM FILLED WITH OBSTACLES.

1986 CARNEGIE MELLON UNIVERSITY (CMU) ENGINEERS MAKE SELF-DRIVING VEHICLES WITH SENSORS.

1995 CMU ENGINEERS DRIVE A CAR 70 MILES (113 KM) ON ROADS WITHOUT HUMAN AID.

2009 GOOGLE BEGINS TESTING ROBOTIC CARS.

2015 TESLA FEATURES THE AUTOPILOT PROGRAM IN ITS MODEL S.

2016 GOOGLE TURNS ITS SELF-DRIVING CAR UNIT INTO A SEPARATE COMPANY, WAYMO.

2018 AUTONOMOUS TRUCKS ARE TESTED IN THE UNITED STATES AND THE UNITED KINGDOM.

2022 THE U.S. NATIONAL HIGHWAY TRAFFIC SAFETY ADMINISTRATION OKAYS THE PRODUCTION OF CARS WITHOUT STEERING WHEELS AND PEDALS.

PAVING THE WAY

MOST CARMAKERS ARE WORKING WITH COMPANIES THAT FOCUS ON SELF-DRIVING TECHNOLOGIES TO PRODUCE AUTONOMOUS CARS. FOR EXAMPLE, WAYMO (FORMERLY THE GOOGLE SELF-DRIVING COMPANY) IS CURRENTLY PARTNERED WITH CHRYSLER FOR AN AUTONOMOUS TAXI SERVICE BEING TESTED IN PHOENIX, ARIZONA, AND SAN FRANCISCO, CALIFORNIA. WAYMO IS ALSO WORKING WITH VOLVO, LAND ROVER JAGUAR, AND THE RENAULT NISSAN MITSUBISHI COMPANIES AS OF 2022.

GLOSSARY

concept car: A car built to show a new design and features that may one day be used in cars sold to the public.

cylindrical: Shaped like a tube.

designer: Someone who plans what something should look like.

develop: To create something over time.

distract: To take attention away from an activity.

echolocation: A way of locating things by producing sounds that bounce off objects.

emergency: An unexpected situation that needs quick action.

environment: All the conditions that surround something.

frequency: How many times a sound wave is repeated in a period of time. A low-frequency sound wave produces a low-pitched sound, while a high-frequency sound wave produces a high-pitched sound.

navigation: The science of plotting and following a path from one place to another.

obstacle: Something that blocks a path.

satellite: A machine sent into space that moves around Earth, the moon, the sun, or a planet to complete scientific research or a type of communication.

technology: Using science, engineering, and other industries to invent useful tools or to solve problems. Also a machine, piece of equipment, or method created by technology.

vehicle: An object used for carrying or transporting people or goods, such as a car, truck, or airplane.

FOR MORE INFORMATION

BOOKS

Fishman, Jon M. *Cool Self-Driving Cars.* Minneapolis, MN: Lerner Publications, 2019.

Mosloski, Jessica. *How Self-Driving Cars Will Impact Society.* San Diego, CA: ReferencePoint Press, Inc., 2019.

Rathburn, Betsy. *Self-Driving Cars.* Minneapolis, MN: Bellwether, 2021.

WEBSITES

Can a Car Drive Itself?
wonderopolis.org/wonder/can-a-car-drive-itself
Consider more of the pros and cons of autonomous cars.

LIDAR: How Self-Driving Cars "See" Where They're Going
cosmosmagazine.com/technology/lidar-how-self-driving-cars-see/
Read an in-depth description of this important technology.

Self-Driving Cars STEM Activities for Kids
www.sciencebuddies.org/stem-activities/subjects/self-driving-cars-autonomous-vehicles
Learn more about the levels of autonomy a car can have.

Publisher's note to educators and parents: Our editors have carefully reviewed these websites to ensure that they are suitable for students. Many websites change frequently, however, and we cannot guarantee that a site's future contents will continue to meet our high standards of quality and educational value. Be advised that students should be closely supervised whenever they access the internet.

INDEX